BEATING THE DRUM

I0164059

BRENDAN PRESS

Copyright © 2020 Brendan Press

All rights reserved.

ISBN: 978-0-578-72797-4

For Pony & Chedalyne

CONTENTS

ETERNITY

Day in and day out you go in, pocket your money and go home. You finish your shift, step out into the cold night air, and walk to your car. You drive slow cause at 3 A.M. everyone you love is asleep anyway. Neil Young serenades you on the radio. You go the long way. Past rows of sleeping houses with sleeping babies, and wholesome families that work hard to give their kids a good life so they don't end up like you, though you're not really sure if being you is that bad. Some nights you lock up and don't leave. After a long hard night of serving people it's important to decompress. You sit with a few coworkers at a table, crack open a couple of cheap beers, and take in the silence. Once in a while someone lets one rip, and everyone laughs.

SWEET SPOT

The last bus of the night hisses by our window. The smell of firewood from the big apartments across the street has dissipated, disappeared into the night. The kids are asleep. Parents with expensive paintings above their bed, fresh, new paintings with line marks and brush strokes they hope will appreciate in value as the days, years, and decades go by, place their reading glasses on the nightstand, shut off the laptops, and try to be grateful for the next day. For the sardine train commute, the grind, company meetings, Cobb salad lunches with associates in pink polo shirts sipping on iced tea, the sardine commute back, cooking dinner, maybe take-out, homework with the kids, baths, bedtime stories, and then sleep again. The raccoons, the newest addition to the neighborhood, who, growing up in Queens my whole life, I've never seen, have replaced the rats and roaches. They're out and about digging through trash bags, hiding behind bushes, waiting for a sign that no one else is out there, that nothing else exists, that they are free to roam and rummage for chicken bones, free to lick the insides of cans for that last drop of something tasty, something good. But they know better. They know that after me, coming back from my shift, the last of the drunks serenading themselves with their lovesick vomit songs have to make it home too. "The city that never sleeps," they say, and they're right, and the raccoons know it, discuss it with one another during their meetings before venturing out for their work. And when I turn off my laptop, kiss my wife goodnight, and my mom, who graciously let us move into her one bedroom apartment so we could save money, and put it toward, "something worthwhile," as she says, is snoring in bed, and the streets are good and ready for the animals, nothing but darkness out there, in come the drunks, stumbling into the purple flowers along the path, singing their hearts out, forlorn songs about love unfulfilled, about the sweetest rose they never got to smell. They manage to get the keys out of their pocket, drop them in the hallway, their heads on the cold wall. And with their dirty jeans and liquor, the sweet cherry woodsy smell of liquor on their breath, crawl into bed with their children and cry themselves to sleep. The black foam buried deep in their feet swims up through the veins, swirls up like the flowers of their sweet spots, and out of them. In the morning goldfish sprout from the children's skulls. No one witnesses the change. No one witnesses anything. And no one is sure if the animals got a chance to eat.

GOLDEN AGE

Some days you wake up jangling, feeling fresh. You hop out of bed, open the blinds, and the sun comes in like a goddamn brass section. Your bones crack, your knees, shoulders, and gold pours out. In the mirror you splash water on your face, and say, "today I will radiate gold. I will be nothing less than strong and warm with everyone I meet." With that feeling you can last a thousand years no problem, and maybe a thousand more. Yeah, some days you wake up feeling so good, no idea why, as if a million loving cats snuck into your room, and licked your soul clean while you were sleeping.

FEAST

Thinking about sex is the only thing that gets me to sleep. When I was a kid the same thing. Even before I understood what sex meant, its power. Sex sex sex dripping in my brain as sex always does in poems. Sex never hops, skips, or runs. It's always oozing, wet and sliding. I lie in bed and put myself in catastrophic situations with my past conquests, the few there were. I'm with this one in a war torn city pressed up against a brick wall on a hidden narrow street that smells like wet cement, the sound of a bicycle going by. Or we're waiters in a restaurant and get trapped in a walk-in freezer, left for the night. What else can you do, but grasp onto as much body heat as you can before you die. It's always the end of the world and sex is the last hoorah. During the day it's all about sex too. When I'm driving, the hot sun burning my arm out the window. At night when I'm playing with the cats, washing dishes, reading a book on the couch. Every few lines my mind goes to sex. It's got to stop, at least in bed, next to my wife, in the darkness, her holding me as if I were an ugly hairy spider she doesn't want to kill, wants to free, put outside in the grass. It's not even sex as much as it's about romance, unfinished business, women I don't have anymore. Women that forgot about me a long time ago. One day I'll lie in bed thinking about my wife. I owe it to her to not reminisce, to forget about the ones I kissed at basement parties that reeked of wet dogs decades ago. I'm an adult for christ's sake, but I've been committed to this sex thing for so long. I try to change, close my eyes, and think about nothing sexual: no soft kisses, no sucking, no bodies. Just me in the blackness. But the itch in my head comes back. I push, it comes again. The basement comes back, the dogs. So I stay with the dogs for a while. And soon they're dead. Dead dogs in basements, paws sticking out of rubble, entrails like bubblegum on the side of a road dripping in my brain. Dead dogs that lived on farms and went too far out to investigate a rustle in the bushes, and got knocked out by chance, by that one car cruising past. A real mistake, unfortunate, that no one saw. Dead dogs in the long grass next to a wooden fence that stretches for miles, and secludes the homeowners that put it up. Dead dogs with their dead tongues and dead teeth, no purpose to any of it anymore. No use for tongues, teeth, no use at all. I can't fall asleep with dead dogs. I go back to sex.

LIFE LESSON

High school teachers are some of the bravest people I've met. Like the Spanish teacher, a big lady with sagging tits, matchstick teeth, really just a stingray on two legs with frazzled hair, who on the first day of class had the guts to tell a room full of horny freshmen, sweat stained yellow pit boys in white shirts, to always remember to be generous lovers. There was no point after that. I should've dropped out.

BLUE EYES

It was the beginning of winter break, and what a prize, I thought, to end the semester with finally meeting you after years of chatting online. This was modern love, modern romance at its finest. I went out to Long Island, stood on the freezing platform with the seagulls and a few old ladies with purses and puffy jackets, on their afternoon commutes, headed further out or going back, squinting in the light, nothing in either direction. Suburbia and shopping malls as far as the eye could see. I never even saw your face, based it all on that mellifluous Snow White voice of yours just hours before departing. Back at the house your mom was quick to remind you of the "no closed doors" policy on account of your brother's past transgressive hanky panky moment, when she walked in on him with his gal pal on her knees. She made sure to periodically check in with lemonade and crackers, or peek in with a basket of laundry in her hands. Your brother came in to bust balls with the "so you're the new guy" speech. "You could've had me that day," you said once we started wasting afternoons in Queens. Except for the dog no one was ever home. My mom was always at work. Hours and hours and hours of rubbing people's faces, hands, feet, facials, manis and pedis, 18 plus hours a day hunched over in a little chair working, while we stayed in bed doing our business, ordering greasy take-out, and going again. But we tried to be polite, never stained the sheets, just in case my mom did find out. Not even dirt from the time I had to walk the dog, and you were going to miss your train, but we couldn't help ourselves, left our shoes on, your goth black boots, our legs dangling over the bed. Fool of me to want to expand our relationship into an actual relationship. "There's gotta be more than sex," I said a few weeks in, and you laughed at me, having never met a guy that would succumb to such lunacy. "Sure let's give it a go darlin'." We went to Julia Roberts movies, drank green tea in cafes, but all I kept thinking about was us in my room, the shoebox room with the pigeons shuffling around in the air conditioner. Of course it didn't work. Nothing works when you're in your 20s. I blamed it on you being too good, too loving, too patient with me. The way you looked at me. That kind of trust can scare the shit out of a young fella, keep scaring him till the end of time. It's too much to live up to someone else's expectations. Last I heard you were working with deaf kids in Rhode Island. I hope you found real love out there. Someone to go to movies with on a Friday night. That brings you soup when you're sick. That makes you cum. I don't think I ever did. It's a regret that might do me in when I'm an old man shopping for canes.

BROOKLYN

When I was six me and my mom moved in with my grandma. She made carrot juice every day. My mom chain smoked and worked all the time. I never believed her smile. My dad would stalk us at the laundromat. There was a pet rabbit there. It fell out of my hands. We didn't stay long enough to get comfortable.

LOVE REMOVAL MACHINE

Cathy's done murdering her husband. She's not looking for anything better anymore, but she's content giving up the task. "There are bigger things out there," she tells me, "than spiking that fucker's food with Draino." I don't know if she knows she's right. She's been crying every day this week. I think she's been crying since the first day I met her. She goes out for a cigarette, comes back, does a shot of Grand Marnier, and then she's ready to sweep the dining room after the European tourists that came in at 7:30 on the dot, 80 or more of them, tall, old and stoic, huddled behind the sliding doors, all at once, all ready with their yellow hotel vouchers and dietary restrictions, leave. It's a big fucker, the dining room, and takes at least an hour to clean, and that's without mopping, refilling jam trays, salt and pepper shakers, polishing the forks and steak knives, and draping white tablecloths over the tables for the dinner crew. The owner is meticulous and has brass knuckles in his glove compartment, so while he's up in the rooms titty fucking coked out hookers in from out of town on business, we do what he wants. We take our time though, change the music, do more shots of Grand Marnier. It's ours. For an hour or so time is ours. No one comes in for lunch anyway except the last minute teachers, right before our shift ends, in desperate need of margaritas. Cathy never eats. She runs on fuel alone. Maybe that's why she still looks so good. After the alcoholic husband, two kids, and a deaf white cat with a flat face, all in a small apartment in Queens, so against everything she wanted out of life, still living the biker bar days in Florida with her gal pal Pam, who stayed in Florida and ended up face down in a swamp with her new boyfriend keeping his mouth shut, and the cops shrugging their shoulders. Even after all that she's still got it. Her jam comes up, and for a few minutes she's nowhere else but here, dancing with the broom, singing with those red lipstick lips, the sun coming in through the glass roof, shaking her hips, the black apron, her tight muscular legs like braying horses wrapped in spandex running through an open field, breaking out of their own bones, pure energy light busting out of her. "That was the one," she says when the song ends, "that really got the asses shakin' back in the day."

COWBOY

The exterminator who comes to catch the mouse that got loose in the restaurant, crisscrossing across the kitchen, says the best way to kill them, if they're caught in a trap, but still alive, is to boil them. "That'll get those suckers good." He throws the mouse in a bag, charges 80 bucks, and rides into the sunset.

CEREMONY

As you get older your toenails harden. At least that's how it feels. Your toes turn to steel, you lose your sex drive, kinda, and then you die. After the ceremony pallbearers fiending for a cold one carry you to the hearse muttering under their breath. "This guy wasn't even fat," they wipe sweat off their brows. They wish the coffin was filled with booze. They think about it for a long while and start to feel bad burying you, because of it. But in the grave you go. The dust poofs up and settles back on the earth. The diggers finish. The pallbearers head to the bar. They celebrate the life you lived and your hard toes as if you were one of the lucky ones.

WEREWOLF

There are no lights, no pavement, nothing. I'm lost and there's no going back. I open the windows, let the night air in. It's so dark I consider for a second the world is flat again. That if I keep driving I'll slip into darkness. Mutate into something new.

EMILY

You think you were a deer killed by a car in a past life. I believe you.
I see it in your eyes.

SHISH KEBAB

The devil was in my room last night. He brought porn, drugs, all the goodies. Everyone else was asleep. The whole world snoring in their pajama hats, and fluffy sheets, dreaming of cream cakes and ice cream sundaes. He did what he came to do, slid under the door, and echoed down the hall. The next morning I wasn't the same. Woke up feeling dusty, my balls like a set of thrift store coffee cups. The years were rolling, and I realized I'd done nothing. I felt that feeling everywhere I went after that, got lost in it. Moping around like a little boy begging for mama. A part of me wished the devil would come back and put me out of my misery. Bite my fingers off and shove them up my ass. Rip the meat clean off my head, and throw my skull on his pitchfork like shish kebab with all the other skulls. A collection of all the winners.

SOAP

There's no more soap left, nothing clean. I stop washing. I stink.
The dead don't even want me, but take me in anyway. Now I have
new friends.

BREEZE

People love scenic spots. They love scenic drives too. A scenic drive to a scenic spot is like witnessing a galaxy merger, like hitting the jackpot. People will hike mountains, walk up landmarks, rummage around inside statue heads just to be wooed and wowed. And can you blame them? Everyone wants a little magic in their lives. "We have to see the view from up there," they say. And then they do. And then they're done. At that point the sun's almost gone. They're tired and hungry. Then it's them, with their shorts and backpacks, complaining about everything, even the breeze, all the way down.

PROOF

People will launch themselves 1800 feet in the air in a homemade rocket built out of scrap to prove the world is flat. That's okay. It's good to keep moving.

PEACH TREE

An old woman who was smart enough when she was young to buy an apartment in the West Village did, and stayed for decades. Now she has gray haystack hair, glasses. She starts wearing overalls. Her husband doesn't understand the fashion sense, doesn't understand what it all means, that it's a change she's looking for. Country life, a slower life that's pulling her away from him, herself, the trucks, cars, and cabs. Away from people, and more people, babies being born, so many more people. People running around the city, gorgeous disaster city, city of history with all its architecture, faces of gods with blank eyes and flowing beards carved into the stone slabs that no one has time to notice. Just people and their places, destinations, bars closing for the night, and the restaurants right behind them getting ready to open. Waiters in white long butcher aprons pouring water for skinny girls in sunglasses on outdoor patios with tiny dogs tied to the legs of their chairs in the perfect weather that only happens in the spring or autumn, when light coats everything with the soft gauze of the city gods or something less dramatic, and forces everyone out of hibernation, or to stay out a little longer. "We could have this all the time," the woman tells her husband. The warm perfect weather, open windows, the smell of fresh air instead, but he's not convinced. There's too much time and money and memory invested. They decide to wait, decide there's no rush, that life is not over just yet. "Hold on a bit longer," she tells herself, convinces herself. But day in day out she carries the feeling that something has to happen, change, shift, deep in her gut it bubbles up. She cries when she's alone walking around the apartment reading the spines of books on the shelf, bored with everything. And so one day she decides, doesn't tell anyone, not friends, not her husband, to plant a peach tree in front of her building, in the little patch of earth enclosed by a black fence which she learns, promotes surface soil, and allows rain to penetrate the roots. She bends down, alone among the people, gets in the dirt, follows all the rules she learned for planting online, and digs her hands in, touches it, the wet damp earth between her fingers, and for a few hours feels it, really feels it.

SUCCESS

My wife and I bought an old house Upstate. There was no more room for us in the city. We love it. We're finally living alone. No friends, no mothers, no roommates. She's got a garden growing out back. The front door is painted red. We've got cats. We've got ants too. They're eating through all the rotting wood. We spray chemicals, we wipe everything with vinegar, we caulk, but they come back. We keep making plans to change the wood, but that requires getting on ladders, removing gutters, possibly crowbarring hunks of it out of cement, and we're human you know, we don't want to work that hard. I kill them. I don't want to kill anything. It's too much power, too much responsibility. But I don't want that on my wife's conscience, for that to be the reason why they don't let her past the pearly gates. I'll go to hell for her. So I kill them, apologize to the napkin the ants are curled up, shriveling, on their deathbed in. I apologize again and again, but I keep doing it. I can't stop. It's either them or us. We're staying, and I guess they are too. I'm not vouching for them, the fuckers, but they've got stamina. No matter how many walls, they keep eating through, keep on truckin'. Wall after wall, piece by piece. It takes a long time.

SPIDER LIFE

The spider on the ceiling is planning his takeover. He's survived on cotton candy pink insulation from the attic, and is waiting for the day no one will vacuum his web. Once he kills us he'll open the windows, air it out, let all the bugs in. It'll be a feast, an uninterrupted life. A kingdom all alone.

MEAT LOCKER

The old man down the street lives alone. The house is big and empty, and the silent hedges have dried out from the sun. He eats cold pasta and looks like Dracula dying of cancer. His wife left him long ago, but he never liked her much anyway. He sits on the front porch all day waiting for the meat men in their white coats, to come, and hang their hunks from his ceiling.

PERSISTENCE

It rains everyday. People are convinced they'll never see the sun again. That all warmth is gone. Old ladies still hang their wet laundry on the line out back.

GOLDFISH

The man shaves his beard and stands in front of the mirror examining his face. "You'd make an ugly woman," his wife says passing by. Even after knowing what she knows he still doesn't think she's cruel. After all, anything is possible, and these are the days of new belief.

GATHERING

"How come you never go out?" they ask me. "I don't need to," I tell them. I bartend, I drive Uber, I do Airbnb. Isn't that enough human contact? I'm never alone. They get lonely though. They need to be around each other. For me the cats are enough. I could spend the rest of my days with the cats, watching them knead, their paws expanding and retracting like jellyfish on my belly, napping between my legs while I write poetry and sip on cold coffee. Sometimes I think they wish they could do the same thing. Let go of the grind, the drinking, the gatherings, and just be content in their own skin. If you can't be in your own skin all the crowds in the world won't save you. But to each their own. Maybe if I sat in offices, took planes to corporate meetings in Kansas, slept in hotel rooms with brown curtains, a funky smell permeating from the baseboard heating system that might be rotting animal, rotting food, or god knows what, if I powered through rubbery steak served on a tray, dipped lonely fries in honey mustard, watched baseball alone, in bed, flipped through cellphone pics of the kids, maybe then I'd be thirsty for human contact too. To sit in a bar where it's fun and easy, to laugh at dirty jokes, to discuss comic book superheroes, to talk about the past, when life was easy, or at least romanticize that it was, is a trick. We were getting through it back then like we are now, like we will till we die. All anyone wants to do is be around good company. To find an ounce of joy so they don't end up bawling, curled up on the floor, like a piece of cold shrimp, because of an old song they heard on the radio that stirred up the good shit they think they don't have anymore, and will never get back again. If that were the case I'd be out there too, making small talk with bartenders, cabbies, telling the house hosts how great it is to get out of the city, and be able to read Nabokov on the back porch in the late summer sun with a cold beer. They feel like they're wasting time, but I remind them I'm wasting time too. No one's curing cancer. "No no no, you're the real deal," they tell me. And of course I say thank you, and smile, and inside, their comments, their praise, fills me up with confetti and moonbeams, and more than I'll ever show. Their acknowledgement that I did something stupid like pour a drink, kept pouring drinks into the wee hours, made them happy for a speck of time, well it makes me the luckiest son of a bitch in the world. I get paid to hang out with people. And still they say, "you're the hardest working man in town." "Salt of the earth," they call me. And when they're really drunk they draw funny faces on their generous credit card receipts, write me declarations of love on the back, reminding me to never change for anyone, agree that if I ever succeed I'd be the kind of guy to show up to award ceremonies in jeans and a t-shirt, a pickup truck with fishing rods in the back instead of a limo. "The one time I went fishing I puked my guts out from the waves," I tell them. They laugh and I laugh, and I'm just like them, but I don't tell them. I'm just as scared, worried, walking around a ball of anxiety, cooking dinner, crying into salad bowls over Billy Corgan songs. They don't need to hear that shit. They've got their image of me, and who am I to break it for them. What do they got? What do I got? What do any of us got but the images in our heads? So I smile and nod and listen, really listen, thank them, the greats, the ones that make me feel like a rock star, pay my mortgage, give me the freedom to write poetry with my cats. I listen and listen good, like my whole fucking life depended on it.

JUST LIKE HEAVEN

House cats have to settle every day. It must drive them nuts. Must harden in their bellies like day old rice, that feeling, having to rely on someone they don't need. They scratch the kitchen floor, pretending to bury food. Hours are spent chattering at birds and squirrels through glass. The world is outside, but they never touch it. Never get to the meat of it, sink their teeth in, taste it, never see the blood of a fresh kill pooling in the hot sun. There's no hunt, no chase, no life. Even the absolute certainty of death doesn't exist. How could it when they witness the resurrection of their toys every morning.

CORAL

I went to see an old friend of mine the other day. Sat on the Metro North eating an apple staring at the river, watching the kayakers, the luxurious houses with big windows tucked into mountaintops, and on the water, turn into the city, my home, my roots, my heart, my people. Looming projects with ethnic flags hanging from the barred windows, expressways, storage spaces, strip clubs, subway ads to fix your teeth, eyes, face, to change everything about you so you can be comfortable sitting among the crowds, your best self in polite society. Last time I'd seen Doug we were standing outside a bar the night before Thanksgiving with his wife and my wife, drunk, switching between apple and pumpkin pies that my gal brought from work, with plastic forks, right out of the boxes, total pigs. I stepped over strollers and toys to get into his apartment. We patted each other on the back like real men do. Even after years of not seeing each other we both understood that hearty, friendly hugs, really any contact, is only reserved, for weddings and funerals. He grabbed his work phone in case he got a call, and we went out on the balcony in the late morning light with gin and tonics, cigars, and a Sinatra playlist. It felt good to do those things, important even. It was prep work for old age, something familiar we could lean on once we were confined to nursing homes in Florida, the land where New Yorkers go to die. There was no plan for the rest of the day. Doug lit the cigars and we got to talking about stocks and investing, his new thing. "If you wait too long it'll be too late." I agreed with him, and as much as I didn't give a shit I did. Who doesn't want to sit back and watch their money grow on invisible trees. It's exactly what your parents said could never be done. After an hour or so of stocks there wasn't much else to say so we let Ol' Blue Eyes do his thing. We sat like that for a long while, until the neighbor from across the way, in a wife-beater, black shoulder hair glistening in the sunlight, stepped out on his slab of cement to water the plants. He waved. Doug waved back. "This guy is always out there barbecuing in the evenings, wooing different ladies," he whispered. "Good for him," I said. "Well first of all I think it's illegal to have cookouts, and either way, I just don't know Brendan," he kind of laughed. "I just don't know where we went wrong." I smiled and shrugged. I didn't have an answer. We picked up our glasses off the aluminum table, clinked, leaned back in his aluminum chairs, took puffs, and turned up the music.

TEQUILA

Most drinkers are happier when they drink. They laugh and talk, and everything is warm and fuzzy. Life is perfect. No one ever mentions the stench of puke on their breath. It's a minor detail.

NYC MAN

Let's face it, I am a city man. I've got headphones in my ears so no one talks to me. I'll never get used to saying, "mornin'," to strangers walking their dogs. I walk too fast, and breathe too heavy on account of not being able to hear myself. It spooks people in small towns. They look over their shoulder. In the city this is a necessity. You don't want to cross paths at night, walking to the train, with the crouched homeless guy, one hand on the glass, as he rubs one out to the 5th avenue mannequins. In the city you move fast to get where you're going. Even if the day has no purpose you walk like you do, like a big city machine gun motherfucker. So fast you start to blur into colors, buildings, pavement, no feet, no legs, no arms, no face, forgotten with all the rest.

PATRIARCH

All day out there in parking lots, braving the element, cars wait. At night, tired, they drive their tired people home. They pull into the garage and sit in the dark till morning. No one even invites them in for dinner.

STRAWBERRY JAM

This is after you moved from a small shit town to a big shit town in order to properly kick. "Drugs are everywhere," you said. "It's not about drugs." You got a new apartment, a job. Minimum wage with repetitive shuffling and filing you could get lost in. Counseling became serious. Blessing checkout girls after you paid, mandatory. You had a designated laundry day. On Easter Sunday you vacuumed the house sober for the first time, ever. Hundreds of miles away you saw your own rebirth, your body dragged out back by faceless men, your bones cracked like pianos, the sound of every god forgiven. This is after that. After cherry blossoms, copy machines, the end of summer. Wet tanned children from the lake on their way back to the moon. All our wasted time. Long drives. After fun, after polaroid pictures of your skinny hands on the thighs of monuments, after eating gas station sandwiches in silence in the car on the way back home. This is after the green flare of the universe began to rot under the autumn leaves in the yard. And you, somewhere in there, the snake nest in the back of your skull, under your hair, growing all along, out of control. You set yourself on fire. Spread to the other houses, the whole block, neighborhood, town, the town over, the county, state, country. You burning in front of the whole world. Heat so hot eyeballs dried out. Wet shiny blisters on people's faces and arms, everyone cooked like atomic death blast death. Roofs the color of tar. Children burnt to a crisp, ash, nothing. And you, there, never being able to reconcile your failures. Living with that in the pit of your stomach till the very end, just another pile of teeth and ribs next to all the other piles. No more sunshine, morning coffee, purple flowers, park benches, beach umbrellas, birds, bees, refrigerators, fries, beer, oceans, laughter, sweaty sex, cats sleeping in the afternoon sun. No more strawberry fucking jam. Never again. Capiche? No more flavor. The ooey gooey delicious churning red universe, its sugar seeds melting in your mouth, on your tongue, a film of it on your teeth, swallowed, filling you up, granules of the earth, sweetness of life, strawberry jam. Never again.

PARADISE

All I want to do is drink spritzes with you in trashy cafes in Paris. To get nice and hammered, the noise of the streets seeping into our bones. Language we don't understand. All day in sunlight with you. And then, into that good moonlight.